Coyote Rescues Hawk

Coyote Rescues Hawk

A Chumash Story

& HISTORY OF THE TOMOL AN OCEAN PLANK CANOE

by Alan Salazar Puchuk Ya'ia'c

CHUMASH/TATAVIAM STORYTELLER

with Illustrations by Mona Lewis

Sunsprite Publications

Published by Sunsprite Publications
Ventura, California

Barbareño Chumash Translations by Matthew Vestuto
Tomol Photographs on Pages 56-62 by Tim Davis
Copy Editing by Jeff McElroy
Design and Typesetting by Ash Good

ISBN-13 (Paperback): 978-1-7358195-7-0
ISBN-13 (Hardcover): 978-1-7358195-8-7

I DEDICATE THIS BOOK TO THE
YOUNG TRIBAL PEOPLE WHO ARE CARRYING
ON THEIR TRIBAL TRADITIONS,
and to the current and future tomol (canoe) builders,
paddlers and captains. I have dedicated the last 25
years of my life to building and paddling in Chumash
tomols and have mentored many young tomol paddlers
along the way. It has been an honor to pull water
with so many brilliant young Chumash people.
Blessings.

Kiwa'nan
Alan Salazar Puchuk Ya'ia'c (Fast Runner)

Contents

Coyote Rescues Hawk

A CHUMASH STORY

Told by Alan Salazar Puchuk Ya'ia'c

CHUMASH/TATAVIAM STORYTELLER

ONE SUMMER DAY, Kʰwitš (Hawk) left his village of Ta'apu and flew to Mikiw. When he got there his friends Hew (Pelican) and Mutʰ (Cormorant) invited him to go fishing with them.

They left the village in their tomol (canoe) and paddled a few miles out to sea and began fishing.

Central & Southern California Coast

○ *Village Sites*
● *Modern City*

Mikiw

Santa Clara River

Santa Barbara

Tuqan (San Miguel Island)

Wima (Santa Rosa Island)

Limuw (Santa Cruz Island)

Ta'apu

Hew and Mutʰ caught several fish.
Kʰwitš was not as skilled as his friends
and had not caught anything.

Kʰwitš tried and tried but he was not
catching any fish. Just as he was starting
to get frustrated he felt a big tug on his
hook and looked down to see a huge
ʼelyewun (swordfish) on his line!

He tried to hold on, but the 'elyewun was
much stronger than Kʰwitš and before he
knew it, the fishing line got tangled around
his leg and the 'elyewun pulled him right
out of the tomol and into the water!

Down and down the 'elyewun dove to
the bottom of the ocean, dragging Kʰwitš
behind him!

Mutʰ dove after his friend, but he could
not dive that deep. He saw the powerful
'elyewun take his friend to a great crystal
'ap (house) at the bottom of the ocean.

Mutʰ returned to the tomol and paddled back to Mikiw with Hew. They went to look for Slow̓ (Golden Eagle), who was the uncle of Kʰwitš. Slow̓ was the wot or chief of the village.

When they found Slow̓ they told him the whole story. Both Mutʰ and Hew offered to return to the spot and try to rescue Kʰwitš.

Slow̓ thanked them. He thought for a while and said:

"I am going to send ʔašḱa' (Coyote), because he is very smart and very clever."

Slow asked ʔaškaˈ if he would go rescue Kʰwitš from the ˈelyewun. ʔaškaˈ hesitated. He knew that the ˈelyewun were very powerful. But in the end, he reluctantly agreed to try to rescue Kʰwitš.

ʔaškaˈ prepared a medicine bag with several supplies he thought he would need. He did not take any weapons. He knew the ˈelyewun outnumbered him and were much stronger than him. He knew he would have to outsmart them.

Early the next morning Mu^h and Hew brought ʔaška' to the spot where Kʰwitš was taken. ʔaška' grabbed his medicine bag, took a deep breath and dove into the water. The dwelling of the 'elyewun was very deep, over a thousand feet to the bottom of the ocean. Muth and Hew waited for ʔaška' in the tomol.

When Ɂaška̓ arrived at the crystal 'ap of the 'elyewun he knew they would be out hunting. Ɂaška̓ cautiously entered the 'ap.

Once inside, he saw Kʰwitš tied to the ceiling. He was barely alive. Ɂaška̓ also saw an old, old 'elyewun asleep on the floor. Ɂaška̓ nudged the old, old man.

"What do you want?" asked the old, old 'elyewun, startled . . .

Ɂaška̓ told him, "My wot, Slow, asked me to come down here and get his nephew, Kʰwitš. I need you to tell me how many 'elyewun live here and how do they survive?"

The old, old man glared at ʔaška' and said "No! I will not tell you anything!"

ʔaška' reached into his medicine bag and grabbed a pawful of unprocessed acorn meal. (Acorn meal needs to be processed before consuming by washing it 8 to 10 times to remove the tannic acids. If you eat unprocessed acorn meal it will give you a really bad stomach ache).

ʔaška' blew the acorn meal into the old, old man's mouth. He swallowed the acorn meal and instantly got a tummy ache.

"Please help me!" The old, old man cried, holding his belly. "Do something to make it better!"

"I can," ʔašḱaʾ said, "But you have to tell me about the ʾelyeẃun."

The old, old man agreed, "I will tell you what you need to know, just help me with my stomach!"

ʔašḱaʾ reached into his medicine pouch and pulled out some California rose petals and made a tea with them.

"Dŕink this and it will help your stomach."

The old, old man drank the rose petal tea and it made him feel much better.

ʔašḱaʾ said, "Now, tell me about the ʾelyeẃun."

The old, old man told him. "The 'elyewun are very powerful. They are so strong that they will grab a whale by its tail and thrash it back and forth until they kill it. Then they will eat large pieces of whale meat, hundreds of pounds at a time. When they are in the ocean they are 'elyewun. But, when they return home, a thick fog encircles the 'ap. The 'elyewun are fish as they enter the fog. When they leave the fog to enter into the 'ap they are old men with long white hair and long white beards. They are strong, fierce and swift. They will be here shortly. You should leave now before they come home."

ʔaška· said. "I am not leaving without Kʰwitš. I am going to hide under this pile of whale bones. Do not say anything about me or else I will give you more of my bad medicine."

Just then a fog encircled the crystal ·ap.

ʔaška· was very scared as he hid under the pile of whale bones. Two old men with long white hair and long white beards emerged from the thick fog. One was tall and one was short. The tall one was dragging a half-eaten whale. The old men looked around their ·ap. They sensed that something was wrong . . . someone was in their ·ap.

The tall old man asked the old, old man, "Is someone hiding in our ·ap? We smell a foul odor."

The old, old man did not say anything, he just nodded towards the pile of whale bones.

The two old men walked over to the pile and asked, "Who is hiding from us?"

ʔaškaʾ pushed his way out of the pile of bones.

"It is me, ʔaškaʾ," he said. "I have been sent here by Sloʾw, my wot. He is very powerful and the uncle of Kʰwitš. He sent me here to rescue Kʰwitš and to bring him back to the village of Mikiw."

The tall old man said, "Your wot sent you? You are skinny and smell awful. We are not afraid of a little ʾaškaʾ."

Just then ʔaška' blew some of his bad acorn meal into the old mens' mouths. They both made a funny face, but the unprocessed acorn meal did not have the same effect as on the old, old man. Instead, it made them toot and toot and toot. The smell from their toots was awful.

ʔaška' said, "Who smells bad now? Would you like something to help with your toots??"

"Yes!" they said.

ʔaškaˑ made them some tea from the rose petals and they drank it. Both of the old men felt better, and their tooting stopped.

The old men said, "We underestimated you, ʔaškaˑ. You are very clever. Join us for dinner, then we will discuss who should keep Kʰwitš."

The old men began to eat large hunks of whale meat. ʔaška' tried to keep up but the old men were much bigger and stronger than him. He knew he would have to outsmart them again. He knew he could not challenge them to a test of strength, for he would lose that battle.

The old men ate for over an hour, not paying any attention to ʔaška'.

Finally, one old man said, "You did not eat very much. Are you sick?"

ʔaška' said, "No, I do not want to eat too much food. It would slow me down. I am a great long-distance runner. A big fat belly like yours would slow me down."

The tall old man said, "We do not have fat bellies, we are stout. Even if you are a fast runner that does not mean you are a fast swimmer. We can swim much faster than you. You are too skinny to keep up with us."

Ɂaška' had set the trap.

"Maybe we should have a race tomorrow to see who gets to keep Kʰwitš," Ɂaška' suggested. "Since your 'ap is at the very bottom of the ocean, we should race to the top where my friends are in their tomol. Then back to the bottom, to your 'ap."

The old men agreed. "Tomorrow morning we will swim to your friend's tomol, then back to our 'ap. The winner keeps Kʰwitš."

They all went to sleep.

* * *

The next morning the thick fog still encircled the old men's house.

They asked ʔaška', "Are you ready?"

"Yes," he said. "You two go through the fog and I will follow. Once you leave the fog the race is on!"

The two men came out of the fog as 'elyewun fish and swam straight up as fast as they could. ʔaška' quickly got right behind the tall 'elyewun and gently bit and held onto his tail. The tall 'elyewun pulled ʔaška' to the surface without knowing he was hitching a ride.

The 'elyewun were swimming so fast
that they both jumped ten feet out of the
water, and so did ʔašká! He had let go of
the swordfish's tail just as they came out
of the water.

As ʔašká jumped out of the water he
howled, "ʔololkoy, ʔololkoy." His friends
Mutʰ and Hew knew who he was howling
for, and they hit the ocean water with
their paddles. ʔololkoy (Dolphin) heard the
howls of ʔašká.

As the 'elyewun swam back down towards
their 'ap, ʔololkoy came to help ʔaška', pushing
him deeper and deeper with her long nose.
This propelled ʔaška' past the 'elyewun, and he
got to the 'ap first! ʔaška' thanked ʔololkoy as
she swam away. He walked through the fog
into the old men's house and quickly untied
Kʰwitš. They were standing at the door when
the two old men entered through the fog.

The tall old man said, "You cheated, ʔaškaʾ!"

"You never said I could not use the help of a friend." ʔaškaʾ said. "Just because I have friends that are willing to help me does not mean I cheated. It means I am smart enough to have powerful friends."

The old men knew ʔaškaʾ had outsmarted them.

"Kʰwitš, you are lucky to have such a good friend like ʔaškaˑ," they said. "You won the race, so you can take Kʰwitš."

ʔaškaˑ and Kʰwitš quickly left and swam to the top of the ocean. Mutʰ and Hew helped them into their tomol. They returned to Mikiw and were welcomed by Slow̓.

Slow was thankful to see his nephew, Kʰwitš. He gave Mutʰ, Hew and ʔaškaʼ many gifts. That night they had a big feast! There was lots of fish for Mutʰ and Hew, and rabbit meat and good acorn bread for Kʰwitš and ʔaškaʼ. They all sat around the fire with full bellies and listened to ʔaškaʼ tell the story. He told them of how he had wrestled with the ʼelyewʼun until they gave up, realizing he was so much stronger. Then ʔaškaʼ just grinned, with a special twinkle in his eyes.

Slow, Mutʰ, Hew and Kʰwitš all enjoyed
the story . . . They did not believe the story,
but they enjoyed it.

the end

Chumash
Glossary & Pronunciation

tomol
canoe

ˈašˈkaˈ
coyote

ˈap
house

kʰwitš
hawk

wot
chief

ˈololˈkoy
dolphin

mutʰ
cormorant

slow
golden eagle

Mikiw
Chumash Village

hew
pelican

ˈelyewun
swordfish

Limuw
Santa Cruz Island

Scan to play recorded pronounciations

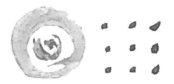

Vowels

The vowels in Barbareño Chumash are very much like the vowels in Spanish.

a — *like the o in hot.*
e — *always like the e in get.*
i — *like the ee in meet, yet sometimes like the i in sit.*
o — *like the o in hotel, but with no lip rounding*
u — *like the oo in loot, with lip rounding.*

Consonants

The left-facing apostrophe is a "glottal stop." It is a consonant and is named after the glottis, the part in our throat where we open and close our windpipe. Since the glottal stop is a consonant, we capitalize it by using the Shepherd's Crook: ʔ.

The glottal at the start of a word is called a "plosive." Air is built up at the windpipe before the sound begins.

The glottal mark above consonants is called an "ejective." This sound doesn't regularly occur in English. The sound is made by building air up at the glottis, applying extra pressure where the sound is made producing a pop, or click, of the sound.

The raised ʰ denotes aspiration. The plain t is like the t in stop, where the tʰ is like the t in top. If you hold your hand in front of your mouth, you can feel the difference between aspirated and non-aspirated consonants.

The š stands for the English "sh", as in show.

Special thanks to Matthew Vestuto, Language Program Coordinator for the Barbareño Band of Mission Indians, for your diligent work revitalizing the Chumash language and for the translations herein.

Coyote's Gifts

Seaweed rattles like the one pictured here are traditional Chumash musical instruments, used to keep time, as the Chumash people did not use drums. Bull Kelp bulbs are often washed ashore along the California coastline. Carefully dried, filled with small pebbles and finished with a driftwood handle, they have a wonderful sound! They are often adorned with earth paints like this one showing a traditional sun symbol (a highly respected sky deity who resides in the upper world).

Abalone has been carved into fishhooks

by Chumash craftspeople for thousands of years. It takes great skill to shape the hard shells and the resulting hooks are both durable and beautiful!

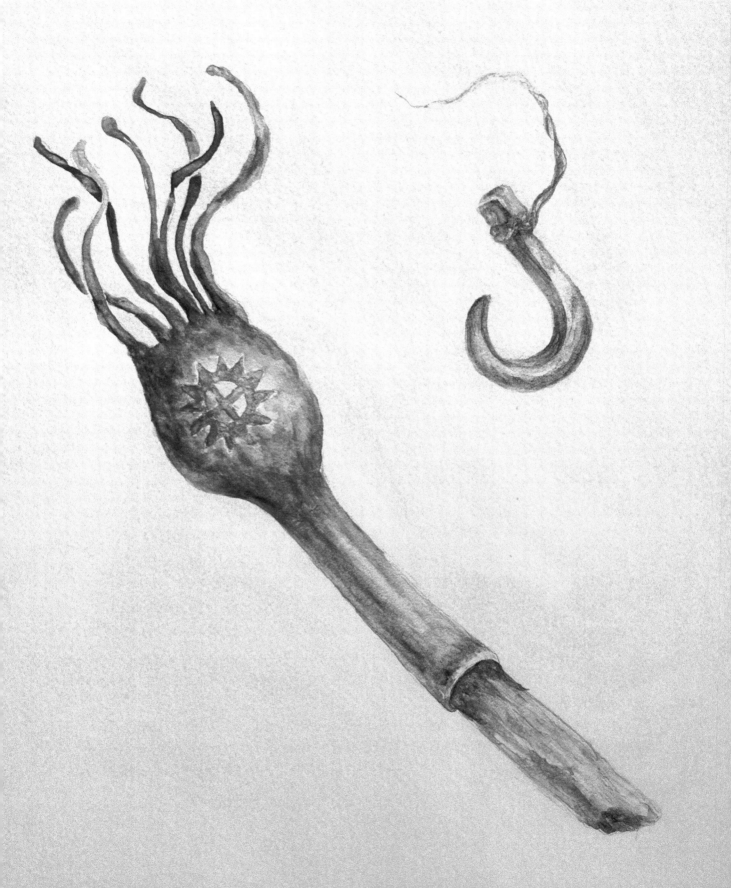

History of the
Chumash Tomol
an Ocean Plank Canoe

I am Alan Salazar Puchuk Ya'ia'c, a Fernandeño Tataviam and Ventureño Chumash Elder. In 1799, my tribal family was forced to live and work at the Mission San Fernando, in California. Tataviam, Chumash and Tongva tribal people were enslaved there for forty years. These tribes had been neighbors for thousands of years; they came together for large gatherings to share songs, stories and knowledge. They continued these customs during their enslavement and many people from the three tribes intermarried. In these pages I will share the knowledge I have learned about my Chumash ancestors and their tomols.

The Chumash people were and are a maritime culture. My ancestors built a unique style of ocean canoe, called the tomol. The Chumash have built tomols for thousands of years. They also built tule reed canoes and small dugout canoes, but it is the tomol, canoes made of boards glued and tied together with strong twine, that carried us great distances between the islands and mainland.

Since 1997, I have been involved with building and paddling Chumash plank tomols. During this time, I have studied the tomol history from Chumash elders, historians, anthropologists and various canoe experts. The following is the history of the plank tomol as I know it.

Chumash Maritime History

It is believed by many experts that the Chumash started building plank tomols about 3,500 years ago. The Chumash tomol builders collected large driftwood logs that washed up on shore during big storms. They shaped whale bones into wedges and hammered them into the logs with hammer stones to make boards ranging from eight to ten feet, or longer. Then, they sanded the boards with shark skin to shape them into what is similar to modern 2"x6" or 2"x8" lumber. They used the longest, thickest board for the bottom of the tomol. The smaller side boards were glued together with a mixture called "yop", hard tar or asphalt melted together with pine pitch or pine sap. The tar or asphalt is still found today in natural seeps throughout Southern California. Once the yop hardened, they tied the boards together with twine made from various plant fibers such as milkweed or dogbane; each tomol required over a mile of handmade twine. Unlike most canoes, our tomols did not have frames or ribs. Our tomol builders were highly skilled craftsmen and highly respected tribal members. The tomols were used to fish and transport people and trade items between mainland and island villages.

Traditional tomol paddle

The modern history of my people, the history for the last 300 years, is well documented. In the early 1700s, early explorers from Spain, England and Russia would be greeted by thirty to forty tomols from almost every Chumash village along the coast. These tomols were between ten and forty feet in length. Many of the tomols would be carrying up to five hundred pounds of fish.

By the late 1700s, Russian and European fishermen and fur trappers began killing Chumash fishermen in their tomols—we were seen as competition in the profitable sea lion and sea otter pelt trade.

Starting in 1769, Chumash men and women were forced to live and labor at the Catholic missions. Young Chumash men and women were forced to grow crops, build adobe buildings and learn various trades. Traditional ecological knowledge, tomol building included, was no longer being passed down.

It is believed that the last few traditional tomols were built by older members of "The Brotherhood of the Tomol", a select group of men that built, owned, fished in and traveled up and down the coast in their tomols. It is also believed that women had their own tomols, which they used for ocean fishing (there is an old Chumash story about the wot's (chief's) daughter fishing in her tomol). But it was the Brotherhood that took trade items or passengers to the islands. During the 1820s, these men were forced to build tomols for the missions San Buenaventura, Santa Barbara, Santa Inés and La Purisima. These tomols were used to trade sea otter pelts with the Spanish and Russian fur traders. They were also used for fishing to help supply the missions with food.

An interesting side note: two tomols from Mission Santa Barbara carried forty or fifty Chumash people who were fleeing the Chumash Revolt of 1824 to Santa Cruz Island. But that is another story for another book.

By 1840 the Chumash had stopped building their plank tomols. We did not build tomols again until 1912 when Fernando Librado, a Chumash elder, built a plank tomol for The San Diego Museum of Man to demonstrate how it was done.

Fernando Librado was a Chumash elder from the Ventura area. His Chumash name was Kitsepawit. His family came from Santa Cruz Island, where he was born. Some of the men in Fernando's family were master tomol builders. The Spanish called them tomoleros, those associated with tomols. They were members of the Brotherhood of the Tomol. As a young man he had learned the old ways of Chumash tomol building. Famous anthropologist John Peabody Harrington recorded 300,000 pages of information from Fernando, 3,000 of which were about tomols.

For the next 50 plus years the Chumash people lived in survival mode. We struggled to survive World War I, "The Great Depression", World War II and the Civil Rights Movements.

Tomols in Modern Times

In 1976, a 26-foot-long tomol named Helek was built for Santa Barbara Museum of Natural History. Helek is the Chumash word for peregrine falcon. It was taken out to San Miguel Island on a large support boat. Chumash men paddled the Helek from San Miguel Island to Santa Rosa Island, then to Santa Cruz Island. They did not attempt a crossing from the mainland to any of the islands before Helek was made a museum piece. It is currently on display at the Santa Barbara Museum of Natural History.

In 1997 a small group of Chumash people and supporters of the Chumash built another tomol named 'Elyewun, swordfish. I was part of that group. I helped build 'Elyewun from the very first board to

Alan Salazar shapes a new wooden tomol paddle

her completion. Peter Howorth, a master canoe builder oversaw the construction of Elye'wun. With support and funding from the Santa Barbara Museum of Natural History and the Santa Barbara Maritime Museum, we completed 'Elyewun in the fall of 1997. I had the honor of being in the first crew when we put her in the water for the first time. It was Thanksgiving weekend, 1997, at the Santa Barbara Harbor.

For the next four years our small group of about 50 Chumash people and Chumash supporters (non-Chumash) practiced paddling in the first truly working tomol in over 150 years.

Our tomols are flat bottomed, which makes them very tippy. To stabilize them, we line the bottom with sandbags. Each sandbag weighs about twenty-five pounds. We place up to 35 sandbags in the bottom of Elye'wun. This puts about 6–8 inches of the tomol underwater, making it more stable. Our tomols are also very deep, over two feet from the top board to

Preparing to launch a newly built tomol

the bottom. To be high enough to paddle over the sides, we paddle on our knees. Our paddles are double bladed and over 11 feet long. It takes great strength, balance and endurance to paddle in a tomol.

Our captains are the navigators. They sit in the stern or rear and control the direction of the tomol. Over the last 24 years our captains have learned many lessons. The Santa Barbara Channel is a very dangerous area for a small craft like a tomol. You have to know the currents and effects of the weather. Winds above 15 miles per hour have caused many a tomol to be lost at sea. With these dangers in mind, we practiced paddling in various conditions, preparing to paddle from the mainland to Santa Cruz Island—a distance of about 25 miles.

Crew members move sandbags for the tomol

We also practiced making crew changes on the open seas - switching paddlers between the tomol and support boat (a rubber motorized dinghy, or Zodiac). The fresh crew members came out in the zodiac. When the zodiac was alongside the tomol, everyone reached out and held the boats together with their arms. One paddler in the tomol would stand up, then step into the zodiac. Then one fresh paddler would stand up in the zodiac and step into the tomol. This is done until we have switched all of the crew. We practiced this for two years.

We practiced long journeys from Santa Barbara to Carpinteria, making sure that 25 to 30 of our paddlers could paddle for two hours or more. On September 8, 2001, we believed we were ready to paddle from Channel Island Harbor in Oxnard, California to Santa Cruz Island, the island the Chumash called Limuw.

We left at 3:45am on Sept. 8, 2001. The ocean is the calmest before dawn. I was the number one paddler. Now, I do not mean I was the best paddler. I was the paddler in the first spot of the tomol. There were three more paddlers behind me, and our captain—five strong, brave men prepared to paddle for three hours. When we left the harbor, it was pitch black dark. We realized we had not practiced paddling in the dark, but my Chumash ancestors had experienced it thousands of times. Paddling under the stars was like a spiritual awakening for many of us. We now call that first crew that leaves in the dark..."Dark Water Paddlers." It is a great honor to be a Dark Water Paddler; they are our strongest paddlers. Over the past 20 years, two women have joined the Dark Water Paddlers crew.

It took us over 11 hours to cross the channel that day, and we learned that the currents between Anacapa Island and Santa Cruz Island can be brutal. First, we paddled to Anacapa Island, where we took some great photos, then continued on to Santa Cruz Island. When we were between the two islands, a strong headwind picked up and we were paddling against the winds and the currents. There was a 30-minute period of paddling that the tomol did not move forward. Only when all the paddlers dug deep and paddled as hard as they could did we move forward. It was at that moment that I realized what great seamen my ancestors were. That is what we strive for today, to be strong, brave and knowledgeable like our Chumash ancestors. After paddling for ten hours, we were still over two miles from our landing spot, Scorpion beach and our tomol was taking on lots of water. Leaks and the over spray from the rough waters had filled the tomol with several inches of

6 crew members paddle the tomol

water. We decided to remove one of the paddlers and six sandbags. It lightened Elye'wun enough for us to make the last few miles safely.

We were greeted by over 150 family members, friends and supporters. We celebrated our historic feat that night on Limuw (Santa Cruz Island), our homeland. Since that day, we have crossed the channel more than 12 times.

For the last 12 years I have paddled in the Santa Ynez Chumash tomol, Muptami (which means "Ancient Dreams"). Our captain is Reggie Pagaling and our future captain is his daughter, Eva Pagaling. We are passing our tomol culture along to the next generation, and our Chumash maritime culture has been revitalized. We are ocean people. We are uniting with ocean people from all around the world. It was a small group of Chumash people that worked on their tomol culture starting in 1997—but it was ocean people of many cultures that helped us bring back the Chumash tomols. That is the story of my involvement with our tomols. I am 71 years old as I write this history and I'm still paddling strong. I hope I can share what little wisdom I have with you in person one day soon. Blessings to everyone.

For more information about Alan Salazar's educational programs and story telling please visit www.native-storytelling.com

— Alan Salazar
Puchuk Ya'ia'c (Fast Runner)
Tribal Elder

Paint Stones
Found in Chumash Territories

by Mona Lewis

Ground pigment from paint stones found in Chumash Territories

The illustrations for this book were made with stones and soil respectfully foraged within Chumash territories. This story is set in the ancient Chumash village of Mikiw, just north of Santa Barbara, California, and most of the colors were collected within sight of that village. These rocks were then ground by hand using a mortar and pestle and mixed with binders to make paints for the illustrations.

Some of the brilliant red ochers were handed down to Alan in the old tradition, from family ancestors who are no longer with us.

We collected other natural materials for our paints locally, including charcoal

Willow Charcoal

Mussel Shells

Ocher

Chalk

Vivianite

made from homegrown white sage and magnetic sands from Carpintería State Beach. This is where Chumash boat builders gathered asphaltum from the natural tar seeps on the beach to seal the seams of their tomols. Ocean water from the California coast was used in the paints as part of the binder.

To achieve the turquoise water tones, I cultivated copper crystals and ground them into pigment (this is easy to do simply by soaking copper in vinegar and water, but it requires care because copper in this form is toxic.)

One color in the collection is not local—the blue vivianite ocher, which I used for the sky and water tones. It comes from the north shore of Washington state and Vancouver. The vivianite found there formed hundreds of years ago as the result of tsunamis that flooded the shoreline, leaving phosphorus in buried plant material and iron in the soil to interact and oxidize, creating the blue ocher you see. The Coast Salish and neighboring tribal people in the Pacific Northwest have used it for thousands of years for painting totem poles.

— Mona Lewis,
Illustrator

For more from artist Mona Lewis
visit www.sunspritehandwork.com,
follow @sunspritehandwork
on Instagram and Facebook or email
sunspritehandwork@yahoo.com

Make a
Model
Tomol

Here are two ways to make a
paper tomol model of your own.

1 *The first is a traditional folded paper boat, with a couple extra folds to make the bottom of the boat flat like the tomol.*

· Use 8 1/2" x 11" printer paper or card stock.

· Fold as shown in the diagram on the next page.

· Then, pull the sides apart gently and fold the peak inside the boat down two times so that it lays flat.

· Cut out the "ears" using the pattern on page 69.
  Glue on the inside ends of the tomol as shown.

· Color your tomol with crayons for a simple art project
  or see page 71 for painting with natural pigments.

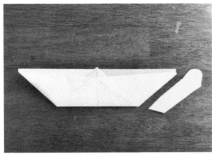

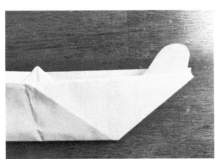

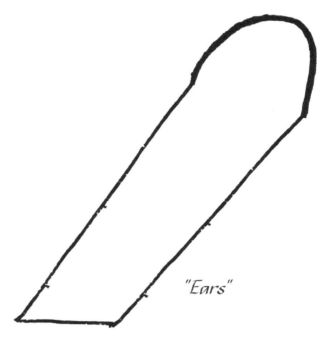

"Ears"

2 *For the second model option, trace or make a copy of the canoe shape on the next page.*

· Cut the canoe shape out on the solid lines.

· Fold and glue together.

· Color your tomol with crayons for a simple art project or see page 71 for painting with natural pigments.

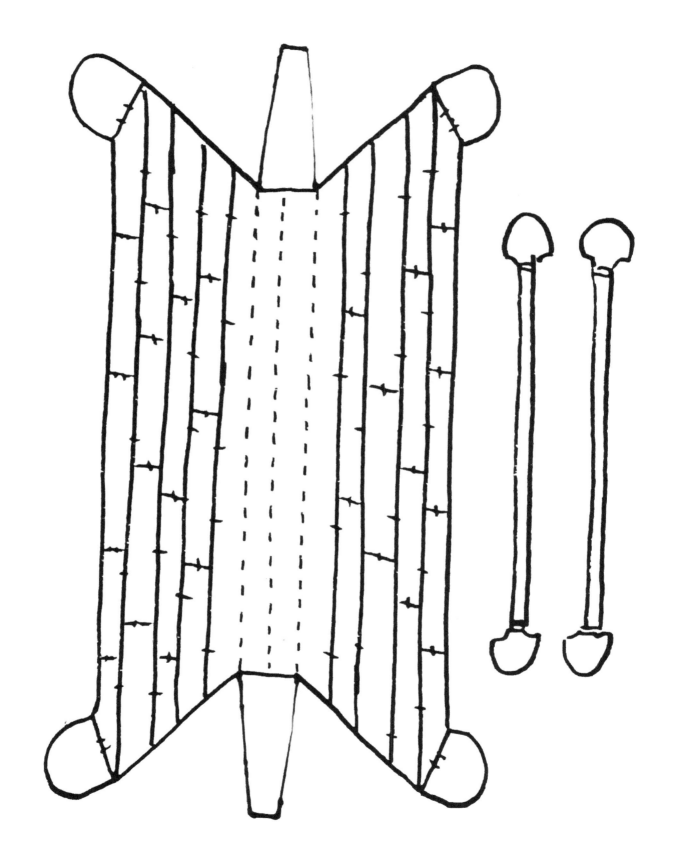

Paint Your Tomol with Natural Colors

According to most anthropologists, Chumash people painted the outside of their tomols with red ocher, using pine pitch as a binder. Since wood tends to soak up water, becoming heavier, this coating was not only for beauty, but to repel water, keeping the canoe lighter in the water.

Ocher stones

Make Red Paint from Ocher

Human beings have had a deep relationship with ochers since time immemorial. Red ocher in particular, has been used as sunscreen, bug repellant, body paint, and as a binding for wounds (it has antibacterial properties). Highly valued as a pigment, ochers have been—and still are—traded, sometimes over long distances, to be used in the arts all over the world. The oldest known ocher paint was found at Blombos Cave in South Africa and has been dated at 80,000 years old!

The Chumash people are known for their spectacular rock art sites. "Painted Cave" in Santa Barbara can be visited by the public, and is just one example of beautiful Chumash painting.

Ochers are made from iron, oxygen and clay. They are abundant and can be found in most areas if you look closely. If you are fortunate enough to live near natural spaces, walk slowly, watching the edges of paths, stream beds, road cuts or cliffs of any kind. You may spot a pretty colored rock. To see if the rock is soft enough to grind for paint, rub it on a really hard rock or the back of a tile. If it makes a mark or the color comes off on your fingers, it will make a nice paint.

If you do find little pieces of red ocher in your area, remember to forage respectfully. Take only what you need and what is easy to pick up.

Then you can grind them up using a mortar and pestle, or even with a hard river stone to make paint for your model. Red ocher is perfect for this project because it mimics the color of the redwood planks used to build the tomol.

Here are some of the red ochers from our personal collection.

We are fortunate to have two ochers (seen in the bowls) that have been passed down two generations from tribal elders and given to Alan for his work. *Natural red ochers can also be purchased online (see Resources on page 79).*

Use a mortar and pestle to grind ocher into a fine powder

Another source for natural red ocher color is by using bricks! Ocher is made of iron, mixed with clay—so a brick is like man-made ocher! You can tell the difference between brick and ocher by looking closely. If you see bits of sand mixed into the red, it is probably a brick. Bricks come in many colors and often have quite a history associated with them, especially if you find some very old brick pieces.

To make a brick into paint, place it into a paper bag, or between the pages of a magazine and hit it with a hammer until you have some small pieces (this keeps the small particles from flying up and hitting you). Grind the small pieces of brick into a powder using a mortar and pestle. A hard river rock can also be used to grind small brick pieces into powder. The longer you grind the brick, the finer your paint will be. Once you have some red powdered pigment, from natural sources or brick, you are ready to make paint.

To paint on paper, water is a fine binder. Historically, powdered pigments have been mixed with saliva, tree sap, oils and eggs, just to name a few of the binders.

For our tomol model, we want a slightly hard surface so the paint will not rub off. Mix the ocher powder with Gum Arabic (which is made from Acacia tree sap). The paint should be thick, about the consistency of poster paint.

Mix powdered pigment with a binder (gum arabic) to make paint.

Make Black Paint from Charcoal

For a natural black paint to indicate the plank seams, you can grind up charcoal and mix the powder with a little Gum Arabic.

Charcoal is easy to make! Just place some twigs of any kind in an airtight tin and place it over a flame in your fireplace or campfire for at least an hour. When it cools, you will have beautiful charcoal to draw with or grind for paint.

Charcoal

Make Black Paint from Magnetite

NOTE: *This paint is for older children and adults. It's not safe to eat magnetite or put it in your mouth*

Another fun option is to make black paint from magnetite! If you find yourself near a beach, look closely at the sand—notice if there are any little black specks in it.

Here are some examples of beach sand containing iron oxide (magnetite).

Magnetite sticking to a magnet

If there are black particles, collect a cup of sand and settle down to separate the sand from the magnetite.

To do this, gently stir the sand with a strong magnet. You can see how the magnetite is sticking to the bar magnets in the picture

Some sand has a lot of magnetite in it, some sand has only a little. Any magnetite will stick to the magnet while the sand will fall off.

Pinch the black particles off and into a container.

Chumash boat builders used tar to seal the seams of the planks. We can mimic this texture by mixing the magnetite powder with white glue at a ratio of about one part glue to one part powder.

Time to Paint!

First, paint your boat red, inside and outside.

When the red ocher paint is dry, paint on the black seams with your charcoal paint or glue/magnetite mixture. The glue will dry clear and the magnetite will look black, like tar.

Paint the ears too! Glue the ears inside the ends of your tomol. Decorate the ears of the tomol if you wish. Traditionally, abalone inlay was used for decoration.

You can use your natural paints to make other art as well!

Acknowledgments

First, I want to acknowledge Juan De Jesus Justo, an elder from the Chumash village of Mikiw who told this traditional story. Thank you, Juan De Jesus Justo, for keeping the stories of my Chumash tomol ancestors alive, for keeping all Chumash stories alive.

My second acknowledgement is to my tomol family, the 242*+ supporters, fellow paddlers and captains that I have tortured with story after story after story.

Special thanks go to Jeff McElroy for his insightful refinements in proofing the text, and to Ash Good for their artistry laying out all the words and pictures to make the book so beautiful!

To those family members who additionally supported this project by adding paintings of their own design, thank you! Melissa Salazar, Eric Salazar, Caden Salazar, Aaron Martin, Jamie Julian, Anthony Loupé and Rudy Loupé.

My final acknowledgement and biggest thank you is to my family. To my kids, Melissa and Eric, and my grandson, Caden. And to my cousins, nieces, nephews, aunties, uncles, parents, grandparents and especially my Aunt Beverly. I love you. I love everyone I have mentioned—I am truly blessed.

Sincerely,
Alan Salazar Puchuk Ya'ia'c (Fast Runner)

* I am a little superstitious; the number 242 is not random.
  My Pop was born in 1924 and my sister Bette was born in 1942... hence 242.

Resources

Support a New Tomol Project

The Patagonia outdoor clothing company, based in Ventura, California, has a longstanding history of supporting Indigenous people, and has graciously offered support for the building of a new traditional tomol for the ongoing revitalization of the Chumash maritime tradition. This new project will be hosted by the Ventureño Band of Mission Indians, in collaboration with the Tataviam Band of Mission Indians.

Part of the proceeds from this book will go to help with the building of the new tomol. If you would like to add your support for this exciting new work, please contact Dayna Barríos at: www.bvbmi.com

Earth Pigments

Ocher and other natural earth pigments can be purchased online at: www.earthpigments.com

Here is a good source for beautiful handmade paints made from natural materials by indigenous artists: www.beampaints.com

About the Author
Alan Salazar Puchuk Ya'ia'c (Fast Runner)

Alan Salazar is a traditional storyteller, a native educator and a native monitor/consultant. He is a tribal elder in both the Fernandeño Tataviam and Ventureño Chumash tribes. He is a tribal spiritual advisor and a traditional paddler of Chumash canoes. His native ancestors were brought into the San Fernando Mission starting in 1799. Like many Fernandeño natives, his family has Tataviam ancestry from the Tataviam village of Chaguayanga, near Santa Clarita, California and Tochonanga in present day Pico Canyon, California. His Chumash ancestry is from the Chumash village of Ta'apu near Simi Valley, California. He continues to actively protect his ancestor's village sites and tribal territories.

Alan has been actively involved with several native indigenous groups. He is a founding member of the Kern County Native American Heritage Preservation Council and the Chumash Maritime Association. He is also a member of the California Indian Advisory Council for the Santa Barbara Museum of Natural History, and the Lancaster Museum of Art and History. Alan has served as a community advisor with the Ventura County Indian Education Consortium for over 25 years and is currently active on the Elder's Council for the Fernandeño Tataviam

Band of Mission Indians. As a member of the Chumash Maritime Association, Alan helped build the first working traditional Chumash plank canoe (tomol) in modern times and has paddled in plank canoes for over 25 years.

The Chumash of antiquity used their tomols to travel extensively between the California coast and the Channel Islands. They had villages on each of the islands, and friends and families traveled inter-island to fish, visit and trade. Alan is one the most experienced Chumash paddlers in modern times, participating in every modern crossing from Oxnard to Santa Cruz Island. The crossings are extremely difficult and dangerous. At the age of 71, Alan is still paddling that 20-mile journey, and has the honor of mentoring many of the young Chumash paddlers, including his son and grandson.

Alan has also been involved with teaching youths about Native American cultures for over 25 years, helping to create educational programs at schools, museums and cultural events both in the United States and in Great Britain.

As a spiritual adviser within the Fernandeño Tataviam and Chumash communities, Alan leads ceremonies and prayer circles during traditional native indigenous gatherings. He was raised to be proud of his native indigenous heritage and takes pride in being a positive role model and a respected elder.

About the Illustrator
Mona Lewis

Mona's family comes from the United Kingdom, France and Scandinavia. She is a watercolor artist and teacher of handwork in Waldorf education since 1996. She is co-director of the Waldorf Practical Arts Teacher Training program associated with the Southern California Waldorf Teacher Training Institute. Mona teaches artists of all ages, teachers and home-schooling families in the plant-dye arts, making earth pigments and in the practical arts of the Waldorf curriculum.

Mona is the author of *Nature's Paintbox: Colors from the Natural World for the Young Artist (and Those Who Are Young at Heart)*, released in 2021, and has illustrated three books for Alan Salazar:

Coyote Rescues Hawk, A Chumash Story
A Tataviam Creation Story
Tata, the Tataviam Towhee, a Tribal Story

All four books are available online at: www.sunspritehandwork.com

Through feather
	and blade, on petal
and soft breezes,
	these stories still flow
through the land,
	inviting us to listen . . .
for now we are
	a part of it too.

Printed in the USA
CPSIA information can be obtained
at www.ICGtesting.com
LVHW070042070923
757482LV00009B/32